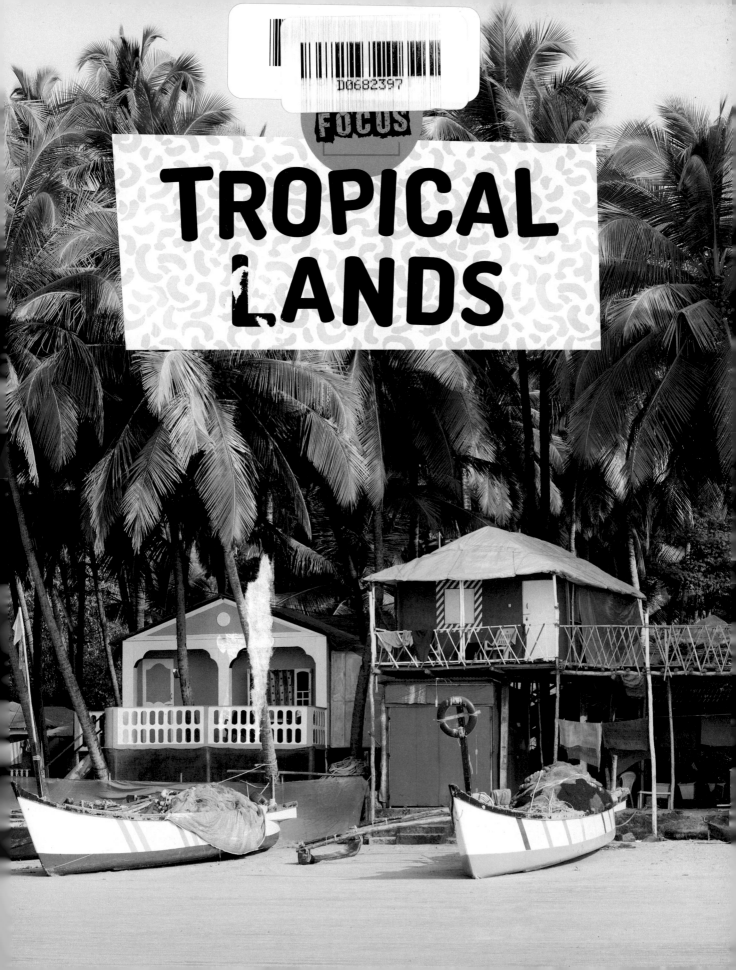

FOCUS

TROPICAL LANDS

First published 2017 by Kingfisher
an imprint of Macmillan Children's Books
20 New Wharf Road, London N1 9RR
Associated companies throughout the world
www.panmacmillan.com

Series editor: Hayley Down
Design: Jeni Child

ISBN 978-0-7534-4140-4

1TR/0717/WKT/UG/128GSM

A CIP catalogue record for this book is available from the British Library.

Printed in China

Picture credits
The Publisher would like to thank the following for permission to reproduce their material.

Top = t; Bottom = b; Middle = m; Left = l; Right = r
Front cover: Alamy/Varun Aditya; Back cover: iStock/Snowleopard1; Back cover flap: iStock/agustavop; Pages 1 iStock/1001nights; 3 Alamy/Juan Carlos Munoz; 4–––5 Shutterstock/Eky Studio; 4t iStock//DNY59; 4b iStock/Jozev; 5m iStock/Ida Jarsova; 6 iStock/agustavop; 7t iStock/VitalyEdush; 7m iStock/pchoui; 7b iStock/pidjoe; 8–9 iStock/AlexKazachok2; 10m Shutterstock/duchy; 10b iStock/LucynaKoch; 11m Shutterstock/Alexander Mazurkevich; 11b iStock/LuiNian; 12–13 iStock/bonniecaton; 12b Alamy/Xinhua; 13t Alamy/Brian Van Tighem; 13b Getty/Australian Scenics; 14–15 Alamy/Kjersti Joergensen; 16 Getty/Timothy Laman; 17t iStock/Hailshadow; 17m iStock/Brasil2; 17b iStock/Marcelo Horn; 18–19 iStock/JohnnyLye; 18 iStock/xeni4ka; 19 Shutterstock/pruit phatsrivong; 20 iStock/FabioFilzi; 21t iStock/Artuch; 21b iStock/DNY59; 22–23 Getty/David Tipling; 24 (1) Alamy/Joe Vogan; 25 (2) iStockhayatikayhan; 25 (3) Shutterstock/manado; 25 (4) Shutterstock/Ryan M. Bolton; 25 (5) Alamy/Jason Edwards; 25 (6) iStock/ChepeNicoli; 25 (7) iStock/Antonio Clemens; 25 (8) FLPA/Photo Researchers; 25 (9) Alamy/Tom Stack; 25 (10) Shutterstock/Dr Morley Read; 26tl iStock/Kenneth Canning; 26br iStock/MaggyMeyer; 27t iStock/guenterguni; 27m iStock/Siempreverde22; 27b iStock/WLDavies; 28–29 FLAP/Jurgen&Christine Sohns; 30 iStock/cinoby; 31 (2) iStock/Aneese; 31 (3) iStock/hypergurl; 31 (4) iStock; 31 (5) Keoki Stender; 31 (6) iStock/Topaz777; 31 (7) Alamy/Arco/C.Lacz; 31 (8) iStock/cineuno; 31 (9) iStock LeaveWithSteve; 31 (10) Shutterstock/Henner Damke; 32–33 iStock/1001slide; 32l iStock/ivanmateev; 32r iStock/1001slide; 33l iStock/romkaz; 33r iStock/FernandoQuevedo; 34 Getty/PeteOxford/Minden Pictures; 35t iStock/kikkerdirk; 35b iStock/Givaga; 37 iStock/WillieErasmus; 38–39 iStock/Jozev; 40 (1) iStock/Stefonlinton; 41 (2) Alamy/B.A.E. Inc.; 41 (3) Shutterstock/Sainam51; 41 (4) Getty/Joe McDonald; 41 (5) iStock/ByronD; 41 (6) iStock/WLDavies; 41 (7)Nature PL/Stephen Dalton; 41 (8) Alamy/Mark Carwardine; 41 (9) FLPA/Photo Researchers; 41 (10) Alamy/Micnden Pictures; 42–43 Getty/Jeffrey D. Walters; 43 Shutterstock; 44tiStock/WhitcombeRD; 44b Shutterstock/Ivanov Gleb; 45iStock/Enjoylife2; 46l Alamy/MindenPictures; 46r Alamy/Aurora Photos; 47t Shutterstock/Bylightpoet; 47m iStock/KenCanning; 47b Alamy/DavidFleetham; 48–49 Getty/WIN-Initiative; 50 Getty/ Martin Harvey; 51t iStock/janvdb95; 51m Alamy/Bjorn Svensson; 51b iStock/Ida Jarsova; 52t Alamy/Natural History Museum London; 52b Alamy/The Granger Collection; 53t Alamy/Mary Evans Picture Library; 53b Alamy/Pictorial Press Ltd; 54–55 Alamy/Shane Pinder; 55 AlamyAkintunde Akinleye; 56t iStock/AndamanSE; 56b Getty/Keren Su; 57 Rex/Stephens/REX/Shutterstock; 58t Shutterstock/Atiketta Sangasaeng; 58bl Alamy/United Archive/IFTN Cinema Collection; 58br Nature PL/Brent Stephenson; 59t iStock/shalamov; 59bl Alamy/The Granger Collection; 59br iStock/imacoconut; 60 Shutterstock/viewfinder; 61 iStock/shalamov; 62 iStock/2630ben; 63 iStock/rackermann.

IN FOCUS

TROPICAL LANDS

BY CLIVE GIFFORD

KINGFISHER

CONTENTS

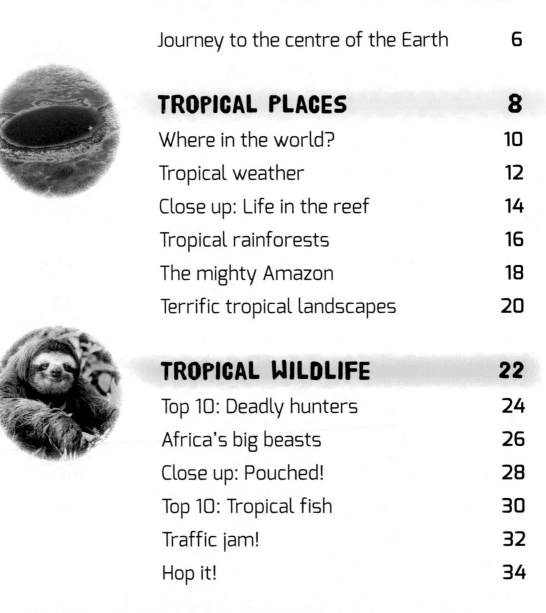

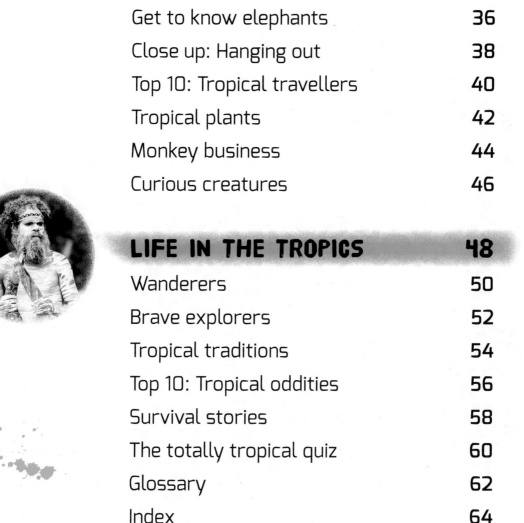

LIFE IN THE TROPICS   48

JOURNEY TO THE CENTRE OF
THE EARTH

The Tropics are a wide belt of land and water that runs around the centre of the Earth, either side of the Equator. They include all the areas on the Earth where the Sun shines directly overhead at least once a year. The Tropics stretch across parts of five continents and contain around a third of the world's people, as well as an incredible variety of other living things. These include the world's largest forests, the heaviest land animals, the world's largest flower and much, much more. Despite being home to some truly wild weather, tropical lands around the planet provide us with much of our food and medicines.

Iguazu Falls, Brazil

INSIDE YOU'LL FIND ...

... **coral reefs**

Check out the climate and geography of the Tropics, from giant coral reefs and stunning waterfalls to boiling lakes and towering tropical rainforests.

Discover the extraordinary wildlife that flourishes in tropical lands, including giant herds of **grazing mammals**, bounding kangaroos, wondrous tropical fish and astonishing rainforest frogs.

... **colourful frogs**

... **fantastic fishermen**

Learn about the fascinating people who have explored the Tropics or, like these Sri Lankan stilt fishermen, call it their home.

TROPICAL PLACES

WHERE IN THE

LUSH RAINFOREST

A hot and steamy climate with large amounts of **rainfall** have helped tropical rainforests grow in Central America, South America, parts of central Africa and parts of Indonesia, Papua New Guinea and South-East Asia. Almost a quarter of Costa Rica is covered in tropical rainforest.

Indonesian rainforest

SAVANNAH PLAINS

Tropical savannah is found in northern South America, parts of Asia and northern Australia but its most famous example is in East Africa. There, you'll find large, rolling **plains** of tall grass and occasional clumps of bushes and trees. These lands support vast herds of grazing animals – from galloping gazelles to gigantic giraffes.

African savannah

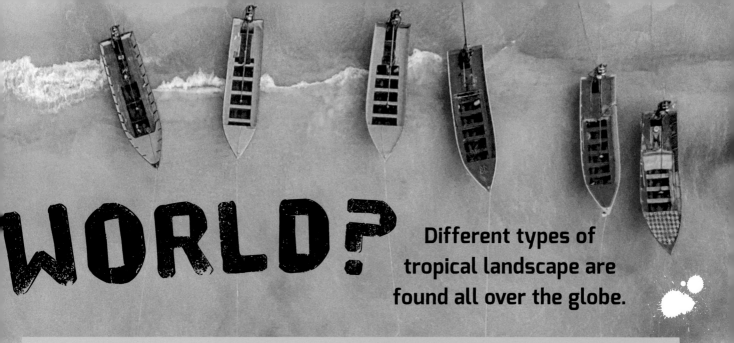

WORLD?

Different types of tropical landscape are found all over the globe.

SWAMPY STUFF

Mangrove **swamps** are found mostly where the land meets the sea throughout the Tropics. More than 80 species of mangrove tree can grow in water or boggy soil with lots of salt in it. They can form dense forests that protect shorelines from erosion (being worn away). Scientists think that mangroves first grew in Asia but have since spread round the world.

mangrove trees

CORAL ATOLLS

Found in the Indian and Pacific oceans, **atolls** form out of rings of coral, which grow up out of the ocean and leave a lagoon of water in the middle. Life on these islands can be precarious. With land just above sea level, these islands are at risk of flooding and their poor soils make farming difficult.

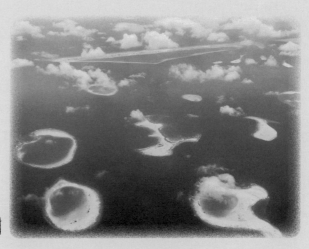

Indian Ocean atoll

TROPICAL WEATHER

Get answers to your questions about the climate and extreme weather that can occur in the Tropics.

How do hurricanes form?

In the Tropics, warm ocean water heats the air above it, causing the air to rise quickly. As it cools, the air gets pushed aside by more rising warm air, which causes the clouds to spin. When the spinning winds reach 118 kilometres per hour, you have a hurricane on your hands! These storms can cause huge damage if they strike land.

Rainbow over Ngorongoro Crater, Tanzania

Which place receives the most lightning?

Lake Maracaibo in Venezuela receives more lightning strikes than any other place in the world! Lightning, created by giant storm clouds above the lake, flashes as often as 280 times per hour for around 260 days of the year.

How much rain falls in the Tropics?

Some tropical regions experience dry spells and droughts while others receive very heavy rainfall. Parts of the Amazon Basin receive 300 centimetres of rain each year, while at Plumb Point in Jamaica, 19.8 centimetres of rain once fell in only 15 minutes. In 2007, part of the Indian Ocean island of Reunion received a staggering 3900 centimetres of rainfall in just three days!

How warm are tropical lands?

Tropical lands boast a warm climate, mostly averaging 24–29 degrees Celsius. Temperatures can soar in summer though. Marble Bar in Western Australia once had 160 days in a row where temperatures stayed above 37.8 degrees Celsius, while at Oodnadatta, also in Australia, temperatures once reached a scorching 50.7 degrees Celsius!

CLOSE UP

LIFE IN THE REEF

Stretching more than 2300 kilometres off the north-eastern coast of Australia, the Great Barrier Reef is the biggest **coral reef** in the world. Its beautiful networks of small reefs, sand bars and small islands, called islets, cover an area five times bigger than the Republic of Ireland. The remains of more than 400 different species of coral form colourful structures underwater. These provide homes for enormous amounts of wildlife and make the reef a popular diving attraction.

Reef life

Among the masses of **marine** life, the reef is home to 133 different species of shark, 30 species of whale and dolphin and thousands of species of shellfish and other **molluscs** – including giant clams that are over 120 years old! One of the biggest of its 1625 different species of fish is the Pacific manta ray (pictured), which can grow to 7 metres wide and weigh almost as much as a rhinoceros!

TROPICAL RAINFORESTS

The Amazon in South America is the world's biggest tropical rainforest. At around 5.5 million square kilometres in area, it's HUGE! If it were a country, the Amazon would be the seventh-largest in the world. The second-largest rainforest is found in the Congo, in central Africa. Around 6 per cent of all of the Earth's land is covered in rainforest – and most of it is tropical. This relatively small amount of land is thought to contain at least half of all the planet's plant and animal species. Tropical rainforests have provided us with many medicines and foods. Hundreds of new species of plant and living thing are discovered there every year.

rhinoceros hornbill

emerald tree boa

HOT &
FACT

Vast numbers of **TREES** grow in a tropical rainforest. They form a packed covering high above the ground as they compete for sunlight to make their food. This is the rainforest canopy and it's alive with large numbers of creatures including birds, snakes, tree frogs and monkeys.

HOT &
FACT

FOREST FLOORS are dark, damp and often covered in **decaying** plant material. Sometimes, no sunlight reaches the floor, yet many plants, fungi, such as mushrooms, and insects live there. Insects provide food for spiders, lizards and ants, which in turn may be eaten by other creatures.

tropical mushroom

deforestation

HOT &
FACT

Some trees are **CUT DOWN** for their timber, others are cleared to make way for new farming land or houses. Around three football pitches worth of Amazon rainforest are cut down every minute!

THE MIGHTY AMAZON

Your questions about the mighty Amazon river answered – including what lives in it!

How long is the Amazon river?

The Amazon river is the largest river to flow through tropical lands. It drains the giant **Amazon Basin**, which at 7 million square kilometres in area is 29 times bigger than the UK. At around 6400 kilometres long, the river itself is as long as the distance between the U.S. city of New York and the Spanish city of Barcelona!

Where does the Amazon come from?

The river starts high in the Andes mountains in southern Peru and flows through parts of Bolivia, Venezuela, Ecuador and Colombia but mostly through Brazil. For large parts of its length, it is surrounded by lush Amazon rainforest. More than 1100 other rivers and large streams flow into the Amazon.

Which animals live in the Amazon?

The river is home to over 3000 **species** of fish with more discovered each year. It is also the habitat of amazing creatures, such as giant otters, which can grow to 1.7 metres long, and pink river dolphins. The largest city on its banks is Manaus in Brazil, with a population of over two million people.

Amazon river

Where does the Amazon end?

The Amazon's waters eventually flow into the Atlantic Ocean off the coast of Brazil. Around 209 million litres enter the ocean every second – that's more than 100 50-metre-long swimming pools! About one-fifth of all the river water that flows into the world's seas and oceans comes from the Amazon.

TERRIFIC TROPICAL LANDSCAPES

Discover fast facts about some of the most amazing tropical land and water features!

ANGEL FALLS in Venezuela towers 979 metres high and its waters drop 807 metres – more than twice the height of New York's Empire State Building!

An incredible 1.5 million litres of water flow over the **IGUAZU FALLS** on the Argentina–Brazil border every second – that's around 10,000 baths full!

Found on the Zambezi river, **VICTORIA FALLS** is Africa's biggest waterfall. It is 1600 metres wide and sends up so much spray that the nearby rainforest is the only place on the Earth that gets watered 24 hours a day, every day!

Rain and floods formed Madagascar's **GIANT STONE FOREST** of razor-sharp, limestone towers.

The waters of **LAKE RETBA** in the African nation of Senegal are bright pink. A similar lake, called Lake Hillier, exists in Western Australia. The colour in both lakes comes from **algae** that live in the waters.

BOILING LAKE on the Caribbean island of Dominica bubbles away at close to boiling point, heated by hot rocks below.

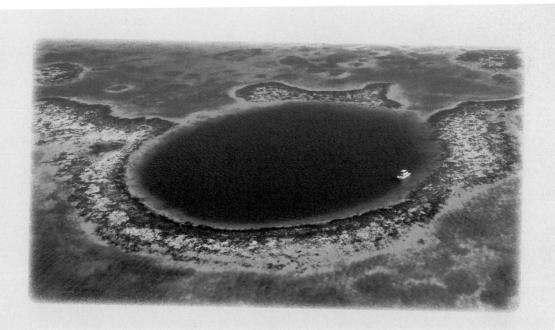

Off the coast of Belize in the Caribbean, the **GREAT BLUE HOLE** is a collapsed cave system about 124 metres deep.

TROPICAL WILDLIFE

DEADLY HUNTERS

Check out this lethal line-up of tropical critters.

1 Jaguar

The biggest cat in the Americas, the agile jaguar can kill with a single bite! It lives alone and hunts deer, sloths, monkeys, turtles and much more – especially the peccary (a type of wild pig).

2 Red-bellied piranha

Groups of these meat-eating fish have been known to eat mammals. Their mouth is full of triangular teeth!

7 Army ants

Working together, thousands of army ants can kill creatures far bigger than themselves – from wasps and beetles to spiders and lizards!

3 Black caiman

These deadly hunters snap up fish in their long jaws. They will attack and eat 1.4-metre-long capybaras – the world's biggest rodents.

8 Vampire fish

Equipped with sharp, fang-like teeth, these fearsome fish are so tough that one of the main fish they feed on are piranhas.

4 Amazonian giant centipede

These beasts eat anything they can kill, coiling around and injecting venom into their victims.

9 Electric eel

These bottom-dwelling river fish can pack quite a punch! Cells in their body can generate a 600-volt electric shock, which they use to stun or kill prey.

5 Green anaconda

This 5-metre-long snake kills by wrapping itself around prey, suffocating the animal, then swallowing the dead creature whole!

10 Brazilian wandering spider

One of the world's most poisonous, this spider's fangs inject venom into prey, such as frogs, mice and lizards.

6 Harpy eagle

This brute of a bird has claws that can grow longer than a bear's! The harpy hunts monkeys, sloths and large birds, such as macaws.

Which deadly hunter is your number one?

AFRICA'S BIG BEASTS

giraffe

Africa is home to some of the largest land animals on the planet, including the biggest land animal on the Earth: the African elephant. Africa is also home to the Earth's tallest animal, the giraffe, and the world's biggest bird, the ostrich. Scientists call these giant animals (and giant plants) megafauna.

HOT FACT

LIONS prey on mammals, such as zebras. A male can eat over 30 kilograms of meat in a single sitting! Lions live in groups called prides, with lionesses doing most of the hunting. Lions sleep up to 20 hours a day. Their mighty roar can be heard as far away as 8 kilometres.

HOT FACT

A male **GIRAFFE** can reach 5.8 metres tall – as tall as a two-storey building! It is the tallest animal on the Earth. A giraffe's long neck helps it reach leaves in the treetops. Giraffes sleep for just 20 minutes to 2 hours at a time.

lioness and cub

mountain gorilla

HOT FACT

A baby mountain **GORILLA** weighs 2 kilograms – less than many human babies! But gorillas grow up fast. An adult male can weigh 240 kilograms. They eat plants, berries and even small insects. Found in central African rainforests, fewer than 900 mountain gorillas are thought to exist in the wild.

hippopotamus

HOT FACT

Weighing as much as three small cars, **HIPPOS** can hold their breath underwater for five minutes. Unpredictable and surprisingly dangerous, hippos could easily swallow up a young child in their giant mouth!

northern white rhino

HOT FACT

There are five species of **RHINO**: three in south Asia and two in Africa – the largest weighs almost 1.5 tonnes! Rhinos are plant-eaters but they can charge at speeds of over 50 kilometres per hour. Scary!

CLOSE UP

POUCHED!

This baby kangaroo, called a joey, admires the view safe and snug inside its mother's pouch. Kangaroos, like koalas and wallabies, are found in Australia. These animals are all marsupials (creatures that carry their babies in a pouch made of a flap of skin). A newborn joey is about the size of a grape and spends up to 10 months living inside its mother's pouch, growing and getting strong from her milk.

Great leaps forwards

There are four species of kangaroo. The biggest, called the red kangaroo, can stand more than 2 metres tall and is a fast mover. It can travel up to 50 kilometres per hour and leap more than 9 metres in a single bound! It uses its long, muscular tail to balance as it moves.

TOP 10 TROPICAL FISH

Tropical fish can be amazing, as this top ten list of fascinating species proves!

1 Red lionfish

Don't be fooled by its beautiful appearance! The lionfish is a deadly **predator**, with up to 18 poisonous spines on its back. It eats fish – including other lionfish.

2 Clownfish

This Indian and Pacific Ocean fish lives in the stinging tentacles of sea anemones for protection. The anemone's sting doesn't hurt the clownfish.

7 Coelacanth

This ancient fish species was thought to have died out over 60 million years ago until a living example was discovered in a fisherman's catch in 1938!

3 Humphead wrasse

Compared to most tropical fish, the humphead wrasse is a whopper! It smashes sea urchins – its food – against a rock to crack open their shell.

8 Parrotfish

These fish eat pieces of coral as they feed. The coral is broken down in their **digestive system** and passed out of their body as sand.

4 Mandarin dragonet

Found mostly on tropical reefs, this fish is a riot of bright colours. Its body is covered in a smelly, toxic slime to put off predators.

9 Frogfish

These short, stout fish come in many types, some of which can change colour to **camouflage** themselves with their surroundings.

5 Stimpson's goby

Found in Hawaii, this fish uses a sucker on its belly to inch its way up rock faces of waterfalls to find pools of water in which to breed.

10 Archerfish

In the Philippines, Indonesia and Australia, archerfish shoot blasts of water to knock out insect prey above the water's surface.

6 Discus fish

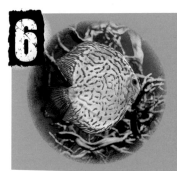

Not all tropical fish are found in the ocean! The discus fish lives in the Amazon river and can grow to be 25 centimetres wide.

Which tropical fish is your number one?

TRAFFIC JAM!

Each year, over a million wildebeest and hundreds of thousands of gazelles and zebras travel across Africa to find fresh water and grass.

WILDEBEEST WONDERS

Between 250,000 and 500,000 baby wildebeest are born in February and March and are on the move with their mothers within days of being born. Wildebeest grow up to 2.4 metres long and can weigh 260 kilograms, more than three humans!

February–March

OFF WE GO

Around every April or May, the hoofed herds move north and north-west, seeking out fresh water and grazing lands. Wildebeests' hooves give off a special **scent**, which other wildebeest can detect to follow the trail.

April–May

RISKY ROUTE

Animals are at risk as they make their journey. Some die from exhaustion or starvation, while others are picked off by predators, such as lions, leopards and hyenas. Crossing rivers can be especially hazardous, as crocodiles may strike!

June–August

RETURN JOURNEY

The herds reach their new grazing lands in August or September and head back in a couple of months. After a 1600-kilometre journey, the herds arrive back where they started in November or December. It won't be long before they're on the move again!

November–December

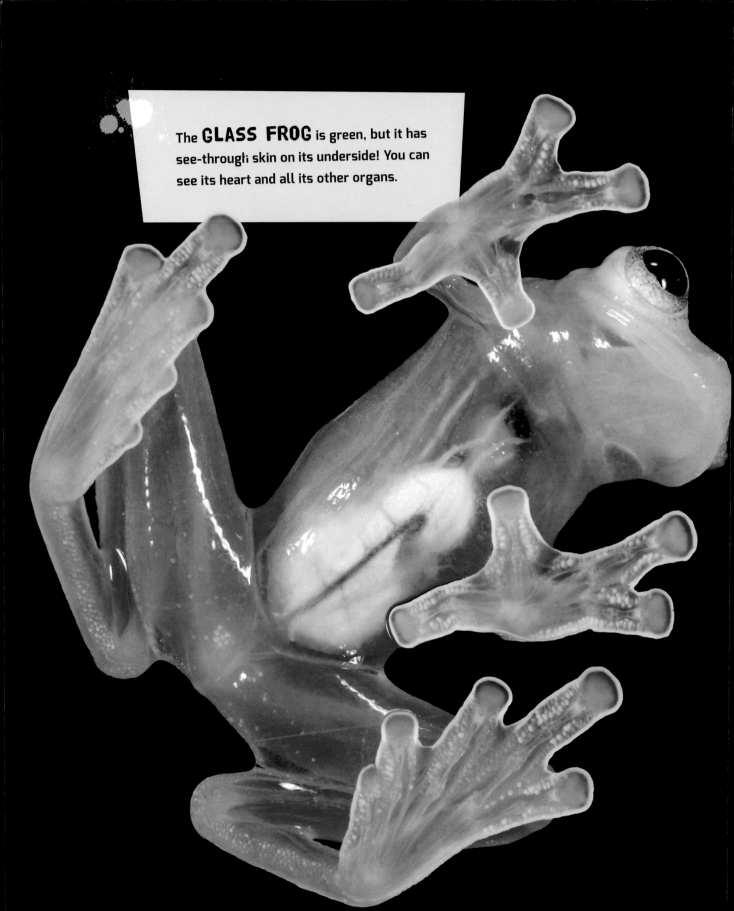

The **GLASS FROG** is green, but it has see-through skin on its underside! You can see its heart and all its other organs.

HOP IT!

Some seriously strange and unique frog species make their homes in the Tropics!

POISON DART FROGS are mostly brightly coloured as a warning to other creatures that they're full of powerful poison.

* West Africa is home to the **GOLIATH FROG**. Growing up to 33 centimetres long and weighing as much as 3.3 kilograms, it's the largest frog in the world.

* The world's **SMALLEST FROG** is a newly discovered species in Papua New Guinea; it is just 7 millimetres long.

* The **GOLDEN POISON DART FROG** may be just 5 centimetres long, but it contains enough poison to kill around 10–20 humans – or 10,000 mice!

* If threatened, the **RED-EYED TREE FROG** can startle its hunter by opening its red eyes wide and waving its large, bright-orange feet.

The **BRAZILIAN HORNED FROG** is found in the Amazon rainforest. It buries its body in leaves and then snaps its jaws to gobble up anything that crosses its path.

GET TO KNOW ELEPHANTS

Get answers to your questions about the biggest land animals on the planet.

Why do elephants throw dirt on their back?

To stop getting sunburn! Sand, dirt and dust work as a simple sunscreen. Adult elephants will also cover infants in the same way and may stand over them to cast shade as the baby elephants sleep.

What do elephants eat?

Elephants are herbivores, meaning they eat plants – and lots of them! Each day, an African elephant may roam 30–60 kilometres to seek food. A male African elephant can eat as much as 140 kilograms of food and produce around 80 kilograms of dung a day! Elephants sometimes use their large tusks to strip bark from trees or dig up the ground so that they can eat plant roots.

What's the difference between African and Asian elephants?

African elephants tend to be larger and heavier than Asian elephants. An African elephant can reach 6 tonnes in weight and has bigger ears than Asian elephants. It has two little finger-like lips on the end of its trunk; Asian elephants have only one. Both male and female African elephants grow tusks while only male Asian elephants do.

How do elephants use their trunk?

Containing more than 40,000 muscle groups, an elephant's trunk is a remarkable feature used for breathing, smelling and making loud trumpeting sounds. An elephant also uses its trunk to grasp objects big or small. It reaches high up for leaves to eat and can suck up as much as 40 litres of water every minute, bringing water to its mouth to drink or spraying its body to keep cool.

CLOSE UP

HANGING OUT

Hanging out in the tropical rainforests of Central and South America, the three-toed sloth is the slowest mammal on the Earth. It sleeps between 15 and 18 hours a day, usually hanging upside-down underneath a tree branch, which it grips with its long, curved claws. When it does move, it has a top speed of just over 200 metres per hour. It moves so slowly and rarely that algae often grow on its fur, as if it is a tree trunk!

The sloth shuffle

The sloth munches on rainforest tree leaves.
These aren't very **nutritious** and it can take
weeks for a sloth to digest a single meal. It
goes to the toilet only around once a week
and clambers all the way down to the ground
from the treetops when it needs to go.

TOP 10 TROPICAL TRAVELLERS

Here are ten fascinating tropical creatures, who move in fast or surprising ways.

1 Cheetah

The fastest creature on land, the cheetah can reach top speeds of over 100 kilometres per hour in short, sharp bursts. Its **flexible** spine acts as a spring, adding power to each stride.

2 Flying fish

To escape hunters, flying fish exit the water and glide above the surface. Their long pectoral (side) fins act like wings!

7 Wallace's flying frog

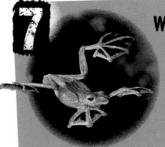

These frogs grow to 10 centimetres in length. They use flaps of skin between their arms as well as their large webbed feet to glide between trees.

3 Gibbon

Kings of the treetops, gibbons use their long arms to swing from branch to branch. They can reach speeds of over 50 kilometres per hour.

8 Mobula ray

These half-tonne rays can jump 2 metres out of the water, before splashing with a giant belly flop!

4 Sugar glider

This mammal has sheets of skin between its feet, which form a simple wing when stretched, allowing the creature to glide between trees.

9 Madagascan sucker-footed bat

This bat can climb a vertical surface with ease thanks to the suckers on its feet, which it covers in a liquid to help them stick to surfaces.

5 Sailfish

Named for the giant dorsal fin that runs along its back, the sailfish is a speedy swimmer! It can race along at 110 kilometres per hour.

10 Namib wheeling spider

To escape predators, the Namib wheeling spider bends its legs and cartwheels away from danger, like a wheel!

6 Impala

These African antelopes escape by leaping! An adult can jump up to 3 metres high and travel over 10 metres in a single bound.

Which tropical traveller is your number one?

TROPICAL PLANTS

Your questions answered about the wonderful world of tropical plants.

Which tropical plants do we eat?

Many fruits, such as papaya, mangoes and limes, originated in tropical lands – as did Brazil nuts, coconuts, sugar, cacao (used to make chocolate), pepper and many spices. It's thought that bananas were first farmed more than 6000 years ago!

Which is the biggest tropical flower?

Rafflesia Arnoldii is found in the rainforests of Borneo in Indonesia and can measure 105 centimetres in diameter and weigh 10 kilograms – about the same as two pet cats. Far from smelling sweet, the flower gives off an overwhelming stench, similar to rotting meat, in order to attract flies. These help **pollinate** the plant so that it can reproduce.

Do any tropical plants eat animals?

Some certainly do! *Nepenthes* (say "nep-EN-thees") – a species of tropical pitcher plant in Asia – consumes insects by luring them into deep pouches filled with a sticky liquid, which digests the creatures. Some larger *Nepenthes* plants can trap and digest rats and lizards.

Which plant grows the largest leaves?

The longest leaves are found on the raffia palm tree in tropical Africa. They can grow up to 24 metres long – longer than two school buses! The biggest leaves by diameter belong to the giant Amazonian water lily. These floating leaves can measure 4 metres in diameter and support the weight of a small child.

MONKEY BUSINESS

Over 250 species of monkey exist and many are found in tropical lands. They range in size from mammoth mandrills to tiny pygmy marmosets.

Found in Borneo, the male **PROBOSCIS MONKEY** has a potbelly and long, bulbous nose, which attracts females.

HOWLER MONKEYS make an absolute racket in the rainforest. Their throat contains a special chamber, which makes their calls loud enough to be heard more than 3000 metres away! The main message from a troop of howler monkeys is: "Stay away: this territory is ours!"

CAPUCHINS are among the most resourceful of all monkeys. They use tools, such as rocks, to smash nuts and rub caterpillars against trees to remove any spines before eating them. Some capuchins have been observed rubbing crushed-up millipedes over their body to act as a mosquito repellent!

The male **MANDRILL'S** face and bottom are brightly coloured – it looks like it has been face-painted at both ends! Mandrills can weigh up to 35 kilograms, making them the world's largest monkey.

The beautiful **GOLDEN LION TAMARIN** has a hair-framed face that looks like a lion's mane. These **endangered** monkeys move their dens daily, so that their scent doesn't build up in one place and attract predators.

CURIOUS CREATURES

Tropical lands are weird and wonderful places, so it is no surprise that they are home to some weird and wonderful creatures! These animals have adapted to live in their tropical homes and find food in these difficult landscapes. Big eyes are great for seeing in the dark, whereas long noses or beaks help animals to seek food in hard-to-reach spots!

HOT FACT

Found in South-East Asia, the cute **PYGMY TARSIER** has eyeballs as big as its brain and can turn its head all the way round. It uses its keen eyesight and long fingers to pluck insects or small bats straight out of the air.

HOT FACT

HONDURAN WHITE BAT

These tiny, fluffy bats – just 4 centimetres long – make their home by tearing tropical leaves to form a tent from which they hang in small groups.

giant anteater

HOT a FACT

With an amazing sense of smell, **GIANT ANTEATERS** sniff out ant nests and termite mounds. They can flick their long, sticky tongue in and out of their mouth to eat a staggering 30,000 ants or termites a day.

sword-billed hummingbird

HOT a FACT

Weighing just 15 grams, the **SWORD-BILLED HUMMINGBIRD** is the only bird in the world with a bill longer than its entire body! It uses the 9–11-centimetre bill to sip nectar from particularly deep flowers.

boxer crab

HOT a FACT

Found in the Indian and Pacific Ocean reefs, the **BOXER CRAB** grabs two sea anemones and waves them, like a cheerleader using pom-poms. The sting in each anemone stuns its prey. Ingenious!

LIFE IN THE TROPICS

WANDERERS

In many parts of the Tropics, nomadic peoples didn't have a permanent home. Instead, they wandered from place to place, hunting and gathering food. Many of these peoples have now settled, but some continue to live as wanderers. There are even some peoples who have yet to make regular contact with the rest of the world, living deep in the rainforest where they rarely come into contact with anyone else.

San hunter, Namibia

San people

The **SAN** people of southern Africa hunted game with arrows made of bone, tipped with poison from a caterpillar. San hunters would follow the tracks of animals for days until they got close enough to attack. They also set traps for smaller animals.

The Amazonian **NUKAK** and **MATSES** people have had contact with the outside world for just 60 years. The Nukak use blowpipes and darts and the Matses use bows and arrows to hunt monkeys, birds, armadillos and frogs.

Matses woman

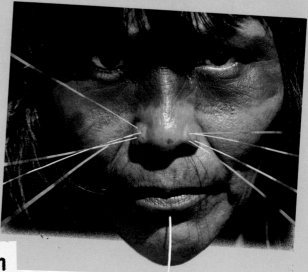

Aborigine man

NATIVE PEOPLE lived in Australia for tens of thousands of years before European explorers arrived. They formed different tribes, speaking over 200 languages. Some wandered in the Australian bush, hunting and gathering food and seeking water.

BRAVE

These extraordinary expeditions involved explorers venturing deep into mysterious tropical lands over two continents.

ALEXANDER AND AIME'S EXPEDITION

EXPLORER FACTS

Name: Alexander von Humboldt
Born: 1769, Berlin (then Prussia, today Germany)
Sailed from: A Coruña, Spain
Arrived: Cumaná, Venezuela, South America, 1799
Travelled: with French scientist, Aimé Bonpland

Both explorers caught the disease typhoid, had to do battle with jaguars and dealt with blood-sucking leeches. They survived and remained excited throughout their journey by the many exotic plants and creatures they encountered, from electric eels to armadillos. Bonpland and von Humboldt found how the Orinoco and Amazon river systems were connected and collected or described more than 6000 plant and animal species. Most of these were not known to people in Europe before.

Driven by their fascination with science and nature, Alexander von Humboldt and Aimé Bonpland sailed across the Atlantic and headed deep into the Amazon rainforest. The pair paddled along the Orinoco River for an incredible distance of 2760 kilometres – farther than from London to Moscow – by rickety canoe. They trekked through dense rainforests and later crossed the mighty Andes mountain range as well as climbing the giant volcano, Mount Chimborazo.

Alexander and Aimé

EXPLORERS

MARY'S EPIC TREK

EXPLORER FACTS

Name: Mary Henrietta Kingsley
Born: 1862, London, England
Sailed from: Liverpool, England
Arrived: Sierra Leone, Africa, 1892
Travelled: Alone

Few women in Victorian England travelled around their own country, but Mary Kingsley went much, much farther! She was sold a one-way ticket from Liverpool to West Africa as few people ever returned. Mary travelled to the hot and sticky West African coast in full Victorian England women's clothing including bonnet, corset, a thick woollen skirt and an umbrella.

Both skirt and umbrella would prove handy as she travelled through the rainforest and canoed up the crocodile-infested Ogooué river. The skirt saved her when she fell into a 4-metre-deep hunting pit, filled with sharp wooden stakes, while she used her umbrella to prod hippos out of her way. She even smashed a paddle over the snout of a crocodile, which was intent on making Mary into a meal.

Mary met and befriended the Fang people, who were notorious **cannibals**, and she was the first European woman to climb Mount Cameroon, a 4040-metre-high volcano. She learned to eat roasted snake and sent samples of new species of fish and insects back to England.

Mary Kingsley

TROPICAL TRADITIONS

Peoples throughout the Tropics have developed their own special customs, traditions and festivals.

Junkanoo celebrations

Many Caribbean islands have their own carnivals. Junkanoo, in the Bahamas, is one of the most colourful Caribbean carnivals, starting on 26th December each year. Giant, brightly coloured costumes made of paper and fabric are worn by members of large groups, or troupes, as they parade through towns on the islands.

Nigerian fishing festival

A strange competition at the Argungu Fishing Festival sees around 30,000 people leap into the Sokoto river and spend an hour catching fish with their hands. The fisherman with the heaviest catch wins a prize, such as an electricity generator or a minibus!

Polynesian palm nets

A centuries-old tradition in Polynesia involves families weaving fishing nets from coconut palms. These are used to form a giant, circular net, called a rau. Fishermen beat the water with large stones attached to ropes. This action herds fish into the rau, held by lots of people who gradually tighten the net to catch the fish and share them out. On the island of Maupiti, this event is held only once every ten years.

Papua New Guinea

The Huli peoples of Papua New Guinea traditionally had no written language. They have gatherings called sing-sings where traditions and customs are passed on through dances and songs. Men cover their faces in bright yellow clay, called ambua, and wear large headdresses adorned with hair, grasses and colourful bird feathers.

TROPICAL ODDITIES

From wacky stunts to curious traditions, people have been responsible for lots of strange stuff in the Tropics!

The Korowai people of Papua, Indonesia live in treehouses, some of which are as high as 45 metres above ground.

* German **HENRIK MAY** loves skiing on sand, and in 2010 skied down the giant sand dunes of the Namib desert, reaching a world record speed of 92 kilometres per hour.

* Some **FISHERMEN** in Sri Lanka balance on a single wooden pole, or stilt, 2 metres above the sea for hours at a time. They fish for herring and mackerel from the sea.

* Up until the 1950s, people living on the Marshall Islands used to canoe around the Pacific Ocean using charts made of **STICKS** bound together, which acted as a map.

* People on Christmas Island have built **CRAB BRIDGES** and tunnels along which more than 30 million red crabs travel as they migrate each year. The crabs move from the island's forest to its beaches to breed.

* People on the island of Yap used giant, round stones with holes in the middle as money. The largest known stone was 3.6 metres wide and weighed 4 tonnes!

In 2015, Australian **ROBBIE MADDISON** surfed big waves near Tahiti – on a motorbike! His bike was fitted with skis and an airbag to help it float.

SURVIVAL

JULIANE KOEPCKE

When an airliner was struck by lightning over Peru in 1971, it fell apart and 17-year-old Juliane Koepcke fell to the ground still strapped into her seat. Surviving the 3200-metre fall, Koepcke suffered a broken collar bone and wounds, which became infected with maggots as she trekked through remote rainforest. Eleven days later, she reached some fishermen, who took her to hospital – she was the only survivor.

THE ROBERTSONS

The Robertson family's sailing trip turned into a nightmare when their boat, *The Ednamair*, was rammed and sunk by killer whales more than 300 kilometres from the Galapagos Islands. For 38 days, the six people survived in a 3-metre-long dinghy and an inflatable life raft in the Pacific Ocean. They ate turtles and flying fish, which they caught, and collected rainwater to drink until they were spotted and rescued by a Japanese fishing trawler.

Koepcke

flying fish

STORIES

ALEXANDER SELKIRK

After a number of voyages as a buccaneer on pirate ships, Alexander Selkirk was left by his ship's captain on an uninhabited island in the South Pacific in 1704. Equipped with a musket gun, a knife and a few other possessions, Selkirk survived as a castaway for four and a half years.. He hunted animals and made his own clothes out of animal skin. His book is thought to have provided inspiration for Daniel Defoe's story, *Robinson Crusoe*.

Selkirk

POON LIM

Cabin steward Poon Lim was a poor swimmer, so he feared the worst when his ship was torpedoed and sunk by a German submarine in 1942. Lim clambered onboard a 2.4-metre-square wooden raft, which would be his home for the next 133 days! He fished, lured sea birds down to the raft to eat and even captured a shark. After drifting more than 1000 kilometres, he was spotted by fishermen near the coast of Brazil.

sea bird

THE TOTALLY TROPICAL QUIZ

Are you an expert on all things tropical? Test your knowledge by completing this quiz! When you've answered all of the questions, turn to page 63 to find your score.

 1 Which country does the Amazon River mostly run through?
a) Peru
b) Colombia
c) Brazil

 2 What is a baby kangaroo called?
a) A joey
b) A cub
c) A calf

 3 What is the biggest cat found in North and South America?
a) Cheetah
b) Jaguar
c) Leopard

 4 Which continent did Victorian adventurer, Mary Kingsley, explore by canoe?
a) Africa
b) South America
c) Asia

 5 How many litres of water can an elephant's trunk suck up every minute?
a) 4 litres
b) 40 litres
c) 400 litres

 6 On which Pacific island did people once use giant round stones, some wider than 3 metres, as money?
a) Fiji
b) Tahiti
c) Yap

 7 Which African animal can hold its breath for up to 3 minutes and weigh as much as three small cars?
a) Giraffe
b) Hippopotamus
c) Lion

 8 In which Caribbean country are Junkanoo street parades held every year?
a) Bahamas
b) Brazil
c) Belize

9 How many ants can a giant anteater eat in a day?
a) 600
b) 5000
c) 30,000

10 On which island do millions of red crabs migrate from the forests to the beaches every year?
a) Trinidad
b) Christmas Island
c) Fiji

11 How many rivers flow into the Amazon?
a) 10
b) 111
c) 1100

12 Which land mammal needs just three steps to reach speeds of up to 60 kilometres per hour?
a) Cheetah
b) Gazelle
c) Jaguar

13 What colour is the water found in Lake Retba in Senegal, Africa?
a) Yellow
b) Pink
c) White

14 Which monkey rubs millipedes on its body as a mosquito repellent?
a) Mandrill
b) Capuchin
c) Howler monkey

15 The poison from a single golden poison dart frog could kill how many mice?
a) 20
b) 500
c) 10,000

16 Which is the second-heaviest land animal after the elephant?
a) Hippopotamus
b) Rhinoceros
c) Giraffe

17 Which waterfall has the biggest drop in the world?
a) Iguazu Falls
b) Angel Falls
c) Victoria Falls

18 How many species of fish can be found in the Great Barrier Reef?
a) 1625
b) 760
c) 340

GLOSSARY

algae
A simple type of plant that does not flower and is mostly found in water.

Amazon Basin
A large part of the continent of South America in which all water from rivers and streams eventually flows into the Amazon river.

atoll
A ring-shaped coral reef which forms a small island with a body of water in the middle called a lagoon.

camouflage
The colours and patterns on a animal's body that help it to blend in with its surroundings. This disguise helps it to hide from predators or creep up on its prey.

cannibal
An animal or person that eats others of its own kind.

climate
The weather conditions in an area over a long period of time.

coral reef
A mound or ridge in the sea formed by the remains of living coral.

decaying
The breaking down or rotting of once living things such as plants and creatures after they have died.

digestive system
The parts of a creature's body that take in food and turn it into substances it can use for energy, growth and repair.

endangered
A species of living thing that is threatened with extinction, meaning the dying out of all members of that species.

pollinate
To move pollen from one plant to another so that new plant seeds can be produced. Sometimes, pollination occurs when pollen is moved between different parts of the same plant.

predator
An animal that hunts and eats other animals for food, defending the group and caring for the young.

rainfall
The amount of rain falling in one area for a set amount of time, such as 24 hours or a month.

scent
The smell or odour given off by a living thing, often used to attract other creatures.

species
A group of living things that share similar characteristics and can breed together to produce young.

swamp
An area of low land which is wet and soggy and sometimes partly covered in water.

tracks
The trail made by a creature's feet or body as it moves across the land.

flexible
Something that can be bent, usually without being broken.

grazing
Eating grasses and other plants found in meadows and on plains.

mammal
Any animal which has hair or fur and can feed babies with its own milk. Nearly all mammals also give birth to live young.

marine
To do with the sea. Marine creatures are those which live always or mostly in the seas and oceans.

mollusc
A large group of creatures, which have a soft body but a hard outer shell, which acts as their skeleton.

nutritious
Describes food that gives people or creatures the substances their bodies need to grow, repair and maintain themselves.

plains
A large area of mostly flat ground. Plains are often covered in grass and low-lying plants although some have areas of forest or bushes.

QUIZ ANSWERS: 1 = c, 2 = a, 3 = b, 4 = a, 5 = b, 6 = c, 7 = b, 8 = a, 9 = c, 10 = b, 11 = c, 12 = a, 13 = b, 14 = b, 15 = c, 16 = b, 17 = b, 18 = a.

INDEX